POPULAR CULTURE

A VIEW FROM THE PAPARAZZI

Orlando Bloom	John Legend
Kelly Clarkson	Lindsay Lohan
Johnny Depp	Mandy Moore
Hilary Duff	Ashlee and Jessica Simpson
Will Ferrell	
Jake Gyllenhaal	Justin Timberlake
Paris and Nicky Hilton	Owen and Luke Wilson
LeBron James	Tiger Woods

Kelly Clarkson

Michelle Lawlor

Mason Crest Publishers

Kelly Clarkson

FRONTIS
Award-winning singer Kelly Clarkson has proven that she is more than just a novelty act, with several bestselling albums and hit singles to her credit.

Produced by 21st Century Publishing and Communications, Inc.

MASON CREST PUBLISHERS INC.
370 Reed Road
Broomall, Pennsylvania 19008
(866) MCP-BOOK (toll free)
www.masoncrest.com

Printed in the United States.

First Printing

9 8 7 6 5 4 3 2 1

Library of Congress Cataloging-in-Publication Data

Lawlor, Michelle.
    Kelly Clarkson / Michelle Lawlor.
        p. cm.— (Pop culture: a view from the paparazzi)
    Includes bibliographical references and index.
    Hardback edition: ISBN-13: 978-1-4222-0199-2
    Paperback edition: ISBN-13: 978-1-4222-0353-8
    1. Clarkson, Kelly, 1982–   —Juvenile literature.   2. Singers—United States—
Biography—Juvenile literature.   I. Title.
ML3930.C523L38 2008
782.42164092—dc22
[B]   200701848

CONTENTS

Kelly Clarkson's incredible voice and stage presence won her a legion of fans as she competed on the televised series *American Idol*. "The pressure is amazing," *Idol* judge Randy Jackson said about the intense competition. "Two months ago [the competitors] were just kids trying to make it." Here, Kelly sings during the *American Idol* finale on September 4, 2002.

1

A Moment Like This

Who says television can't make dreams come true? Certainly not Kelly Clarkson. The girl from the small town of Burleson, Texas, will tell you differently. By competing in the first *American Idol* Kelly realized her desire of becoming a star—and she had her best friend to thank for the fact that she entered the competition in the first place.

American Idol Airs

In the spring of 2002, FOX Network's new television program held open nationwide **auditions** for its new show. Average Americans—each trying to win a chance at fifteen minutes of fame—tried out by singing before a panel of judges. The winner of the competition would receive the coveted prize of a $1 million dollar RCA Records recording contract. Thirty singers who made the initial cuts moved on to the final round of televised competitions, held in Hollywood.

American Idol: The Search for a Superstar, which first aired in June, was an Americanized adaptation of a British television show called "**Pop** Idol." During each week, program celebrity judges critiqued the performances and gave the hopeful singers tips on how to improve. Judges Randy Jackson, a musician and record producer; Paula Abdul, a former pop star; and Simon Cowell, an artist and repertoire representative for Sony BMG Music Entertainment in the United Kingdom provided colorful commentary throughout the competition. Often Cowell would deliver harsh criticisms to the performers that elicited boo's from the crowd. His blunt and sometimes rude comments soon made him the judge America loved to hate.

During the first few episodes of the show, viewers got to see a cross-section of the thousands of applicants from the various cities where *Idol* had held auditions. While some of these contestants lacked the most basic musical ability, others managed to validate themselves. Whether it was for their performances or to scowl at Simon, millions of viewers tuned in each night to watch. They then voted via telephone for their favorite performers—the one with the fewest votes was booted off the show. From its very beginning, *American Idol* was a top-rated show.

The *American Idol* Craze

Over the course of 13 weeks of *Idol* competition, Kelly Clarkson was a crowd favorite, winning over America's hearts with her girl-next-door charm and amazing vocal ability. Her dynamic performances and selection of songs (many made famous by superstars Aretha Franklin and Bette Midler) ensured her survival each week. Kelly watched her competitors pack their bags and go home as she advanced through each round successfully, thanks to America's votes. However, the weeks of competitive singing took their toll. In the final rounds, Kelly's stressed-out, overworked voice could be soothed only by gulping down olive oil before singing.

By the fall of 2002, the *American Idol* craze had swept the nation. Of the original 10,000 applicants, and the 30 semi-finalists who had competed during the television broadcasts, just two finalists remained. On September 3, 2002, a somewhat raspy and exhausted Kelly Clarkson battled Justin Guarini in a final showdown televised live from Hollywood, California. Afterward the voting was left up to the viewers at home.

American Idol **finalists Kelly (left) and Justin Guarini perform during the final episode. Early in the season, Kelly's talent was somewhat overlooked—"Nobody picked up on Kelly until the final 10," commented judge Simon Cowell—but at the end of the show she won a clear victory over Guarini, receiving 58 percent of the audience vote.**

The Grand Finale

The two-hour finale episode aired on September 4, 2002. It featured silly skits and behind-the-scenes footage of both finalists in their hometowns. Americans were given a bit more information about this "girl next door" whose big dreams had led her to *American Idol.* It was not until the very end of the final episode that the television audience learned the voting results. More than 18.2 million viewers had participated, and they gave the 20-year-old singer 58 percent of the votes.

When the results were first announced Kelly admits that she was stunned. She told Reuters:

"I didn't actually hear them actually say I won. . . Justin hugged me and he said congratulations, because the audience got so loud. So I'm kind of like, I'm just standing there. I wonder how it looked, I don't know. But you know you're the winner and I'm like duh, you know."

Guarini was gracious in his defeat. After the final broadcast of competition, he would tell the Associated Press:

"Kelly Clarkson deserves it. . . . I can't sing those songs nearly as good as she can, believe me. And those are hers, and I couldn't be happier because she deserves it."

Smiling from ear to ear and blinking back tears of joy, Kelly accepted her win amid an indoor display of fireworks and the background music of a full choir. She tried to stifle her tears and sing the lyrics, "I can't believe this is happening to me," from her soon-to-be-released **single** "A Moment Like This." But Kelly was so emotionally overwhelmed that she flubbed a few lines. The song, written specifically for the show's finale, fit her situation perfectly. She had never expected anything like this to ever happen to her. But the success was a dream come true, and an event that would change her life forever.

Amid a snowstorm of confetti pouring from the ceiling and in the embrace of the rest of her *Idol* contestants, Kelly finished her winning

Although *American Idol* had not been expected to draw a large audience, the show soon took off. By September 2002, 100 million people had phoned to register their votes, and 23 million people tuned in to watch the finale. Here, many of the participants in the show congratulate Kelly on her victory.

song. All the members of the audience were on their feet, cheering at a fever pitch. This moment, just as the song says, would be exactly what Kelly had waited and hoped for, through so many years. It was a tremendous accomplishment, but was only the beginning for the hardworking and gifted young singer.

One reason for Kelly's popularity is her straightforward, down-to-earth attitude. "I just try to be as real as I can be," she told the *Houston Chronicle* in 2002, "the kind of person who doesn't really care if she is caught without makeup, not some ultra-professional musician who is only 'on' when in front of the camera."

2

Just a Girl from Texas

On April 24, 1982, Jeanne Ann Rose and Stephen Michael Clarkson welcomed their daughter Kelly Brianne Clarkson into the world. Jeanne, an elementary school teacher, and Steve, a car salesman, lived in Fort Worth, Texas, with their two other children, Jason, who turned nine that year, and Alyssa, who turned six.

Split Apart

Six years later, Kelly's parents divorced. They had been together for 17 years, and the split was difficult for Kelly, because it changed her home life drastically. Kelly told *Teen People:*

> **"My brother went with my dad, my sister went with my aunt, and I stayed with my mom. She's the one who got burned in that situation—financially and everything."**

Money was a constant concern for Kelly's mother. She and Kelly had to move around quite a bit so that Jeanne could find work, although they eventually settled down in Burleson, Texas, a suburb of Forth Worth. In 1991, when Kelly was nine years old, her mother married Jimmy Taylor, a building contractor.

Change Has Its Benefits

With all the changes going on in her life, Kelly turned to music as a way to cope with her feelings. Kelly told *Texas Monthly* that she was singing so much that her friend Ashley bought her a **karaoke** machine and put a sign on her closet door that read "Kelly's Recording Studio." Ashley was the sole witness to several impromptu "concert" performances held in Kelly's room.

Although the family changes were tough for Kelly, she ended up being exposed to many different musical influences as a result. And she learned to embrace many different styles of music. Kelly explained to *MTV News*:

> **"My stepfather is into Willie Nelson and Elvis [Presley]. . . . and my real father is into Mariah [Carey] and Whitney [Houston] and Aretha [Franklin]. . . . My mom is into . . . Celine Dion, Barbra [Streisand], Bette [Midler]. . . . And then my brother is a big influence on me. . . . so I grew up loving Guns N'Roses . . . Metallica. . . . I love Aerosmith and No Doubt. I have so many influences on me that are so different. And even country. I love Reba McEntire."**

Discovering Her Talent

When Kelly was in seventh grade at Pauline Hughes Middle School, the school's choir director, Cindy Glenn, overheard the young girl singing to herself one day in the hallway. She urged Kelly to try out for the choir, and although she had never had formal singing lessons, Kelly immediately stood out. She could hit notes that no one else could. Kelly learned a lot from her choir teacher, whom she has thanked for giving her classical training in music. She also credits her teacher for pushing her to do her best.

When Kelly entered Burleson High School in 1996, she joined the choir. Money was tight so she couldn't always afford to pay when the choir traveled to various competitions. But the choir's booster club, her friends, and supportive teachers all contributed funds so that Kelly could participate along with everyone else. She earned a spot on the prestigious Texas All-State Choir, which features only the best singers from high schools around the state. While in high school Kelly actually

Kelly has said that she turned to music in order to deal with the stresses in her life. She found that singing was a good outlet, and that she had a good voice. When she was in high school in Texas, she was chosen for a spot in the prestigious state choir.

sang in three different choirs, and she was also involved in drama, athletics, and the student council.

Outside school, Kelly wrote songs about things going on in her life, and she practiced recording them on her karaoke machine. Kelly told *Teen People*:

> **"The first song I wrote was "Because of You" when I was 16. I had so many issues, coming from a divorced family. Writing is how I got those feelings out. It's like therapy for free!"**

In addition to performing in her school productions of *Brigadoon* and *Seven Brides for Seven Brothers*, Kelly also sang in her hometown church. One Sunday, after singing "Amazing Grace" at church, Kelly was approached by an elderly man. He had some fateful words that had a great effect on her, she told *Inside Connection*:

> **"He said 'God has chosen you and given you the talent, and you're going to go far with this. You've inspired me; this is your way of expressing God's love to people.' That's gotten me through the hard times— remembering that it was God's intent and plan for me, because trust me, I have no other talents! . . . I don't see why I would be blessed with a gift like this one and not use it."**

Breaking into the Biz

After Kelly graduated from high school in 2000, most of her friends went away to college. Kelly continued to live at home with her mother and work on her music. She told *Texas Monthly*:

> **"I didn't want to go to college. My goal was to be a major recording artist. And when I told my mom, she never once discouraged me. She said, 'Kelly, you can do it.'"**

To start her music career, Kelly needed to make a **demo** tape to send to record companies and producers. However, making a demo was expensive. Kelly worked several jobs—at a local zoo, a pharmacy, and a restaurant. She even sang at the amusement park Six Flags over Arlington. Although she made enough to support herself, it wasn't enough for the demo. However, her best friend, Jessica Huggins, helped her out by providing the needed money.

Going West

Once her demo was completed, Kelly and a co-worker from the amusement park left Burleson and moved to Los Angeles, California, where Kelly hoped to break into the music business. She sent her tape to various record companies and went to many auditions, but she received no serious offers. In an interview with *Teen Tribute*, Kelly talked about having to deal with rejection:

During *American Idol* many people were surprised to hear Kelly's powerful voice. "Clarkson stands a mere 5 feet 4 inches, yet her belting, soulful style brings to mind such towers of singing prowess as Etta James and Ethel Merman," wrote *Houston Chronicle* journalist Andrew Marton in an article before the *American Idol* finale.

"I've had many doors slammed in my face. When people say, 'You're not what we're looking for,' you say, 'Well, I am what somebody else is looking for. I've just gotta find them."

Living in LA was expensive, and Kelly had to work several jobs to make ends meet. No stranger to hard work and long hours, she found a job as a waitress and as an extra (earning $50 a day) on several television shows, such as *Dharma & Greg, The Bernie Mac Show, That '70's Show,* and *Sabrina The Teenage Witch.*

After graduating from high school, Kelly recorded a tape of several songs and moved to Los Angeles hoping to pursue her dream of a music career. However, although she went on many auditions, she was unable to convince record company executives to give her a chance. Eventually, Kelly decided to return home to Texas.

Her First Break

Kelly finally caught a break when the well-known songwriter Gerry Goffin gave her work. Goffin is famous for writing "(You Make Me Feel Like) A Natural Woman," written for Aretha Franklin, and "Saving All My Love For You," for Whitney Houston. Through Goffin, Kelly had the opportunity to learn about songwriting and recording techniques.

While in California, Kelly also got the chance to spend time with her father, who lived in the Los Angeles area. She hadn't seen much of him since the divorce and was happy to reestablish a relationship with him.

However, Goffin suddenly fell ill and Kelly no longer had a job. Soon after, her apartment caught fire and burned to the ground. Having lost her apartment and possessions just four months after arriving in LA, Kelly decided it was time to make the long drive back home to Burleson.

Back Home Again

But Kelly was not giving up. She knew that singing was her future, one way or another, whether she performed in Los Angeles or Burleson. One day Kelly learned from her friend Jessica about a new **reality TV** show that was looking for singers. The show was *American Idol*. In the spring of 2002 its producers were holding open auditions in cities across the country, including Dallas, Texas, which was only 40 miles from Burleson.

Jessica even filled out the application forms for Kelly. All she had to do was sign them and show up for the audition. At first Kelly was a bit reluctant about auditioning, but Jessica, believing in her friend, kept pressing. Kelly finally agreed.

The audition was scheduled for early morning, because Kelly had to work one of her many jobs later that afternoon. She was so terrified that she would oversleep and miss the audition that the night before the big day she never went to bed. As a result she was the one to wake up a very surprised Jessica by throwing rocks at *her* window at 4 A.M. That morning, Kelly was the very first person in line for the *Idol* auditions.

The *Idol* judges selected only eleven contestants from Dallas. But Kelly was one of them. She subsequently battled her way through several rounds of auditions and thirteen weeks of intense televised competition to become the first *American Idol*. Afterward, she was ready to show the world what she could do.

Winning *American Idol* made Kelly an instant celebrity. She was in demand on talk shows and for many events. Here, she sings the national anthem on the steps of the Lincoln Memorial for the United Day of Service, a tribute to those who had died in the September 11, 2001, terrorist attacks on the United States.

3

Busy from the Start

After winning the American Idol crown, Kelly Clarkson embarked on a whirlwind of appearances and performances all over the United States. She faced a firestorm of media pressures and an extremely hectic touring schedule. The wheels had been set in motion, and Kelly had to hold on tight to keep up the crazy pace.

A Hectic Schedule

The two weeks following the final broadcast of the first *Idol* competition were busy ones. Kelly traveled to Washington, D.C., where she sang the national anthem at the Lincoln

Memorial. The event was part of the one-year anniversary ceremony of the September 11, 2001, terrorist attacks. Three days later, Kelly made a guest appearance on Fox's comedy series *MAD TV*. And three days after that, RCA issued her very first single, "Before Your Love/A Moment Like This."

"[Kelly's] fame is an authentic product of popular taste," wrote *New York Times* reporter Alex Kuczynski after Kelly won on the first season of *American Idol*. "The audience was charmed by her wholesome looks, her talent and her [refusal to wear] the Britney Spears-clone outfits that other contestants wore like a uniform."

At the end of September, Kelly flew to Las Vegas with the top 30 *Idol* contestants for the filming of a television special entitled "American Idols in Las Vegas." When the television special was broadcast, it included Kelly's music video for "Before Your Love/A Moment Like This." Seven days after the Vegas special, Kelly hit the road for a six-week, 28-city arena tour featuring the top 10 *Idol* finalists.

Kelly's single turned out to be a smash hit. According to the record sales tracking system SoundScan, "Before Your Love/A Moment Like This" sold more than 236,000 copies in its very first week. It set a record for largest jump on the Billboard Hot 100 chart—rocketing from number 52 to number one in just one week. The first week of its release, the song was the number one single in every market in the United States.

And Kelly had more songs coming. On October 1, 2002, the *American Idol: Greatest Moments* album was released. Four of the 15 tracks performed by the show's contestants were Kelly's. Two were Aretha Franklin covers "Respect" and "(You Make Me Feel Like A) Natural Woman" and two were the songs off her **debut** single—"Before Your Love/A Moment Like This."

Behind the Scenes

Everything seemed to be going according to plan. Kelly was busy performing and riding high on the wave of her newfound fame, and her record label, RCA, was raking in the profits. The release of the single and album were all part of a well designed plan.

The creator and producer of *American Idol* was 19 Entertainment, a company founded by Simon Fuller. It had the rights to manage whoever won the TV competition. While the program was still in its final weeks, executives at RCA and 19 Entertainment were busy organizing producers and songwriters to work with the finalist so the companies could capitalize on the show's massive success.

A Singer and Songwriter

After Kelly won, the producers at RCA wanted her to make an album right away. They wanted her music to come out while she was still fresh in viewers' minds.

Kelly, however, had other plans. She didn't want to be rushed into making an album that she wasn't excited about or proud of. She had her own ideas about how she wanted to present herself to the world. And she wanted to write her own material, not simply sing other people's songs. She told the *Dallas Morning News*:

> **"I met with Simon (Fuller) and told him I couldn't put out a CD that soon. There was no way it could be a representation of me. He said, 'I understand perfectly. Let's wait until you get the right material.' So he was actually very cool about it, which I didn't know would happen. You hear a lot about how people push you around and try to make you do stuff you don't want to do. And that was totally not the case."**

The date of release of Kelly's debut album, originally slated for November 26, 2003, was pushed back. And it was decided that Kelly would get writing credits on three of the songs on the new album.

During the process of recording her first album, Kelly was keeping an insanely busy schedule. She was balancing her recording studio sessions with various public appearances, as well as with the filming of her new movie. *From Justin to Kelly: The Rise of Two American Idols* starred Kelly and her *Idol* co-finalist, Justin Guarini. Its plot revolves about two teenagers, Kelly and Justin, who meet on spring break in Miami. The film includes several musical numbers.

The movie's shooting schedule required that it be completed in just six weeks. And when she wasn't filming, Kelly would go back into the studio to record. With all she was doing, Kelly sometimes logged in 20-hour days. However, in interviews she shrugged off the intense schedule, saying that she really didn't feel that much pressure.

Thankful

Once the recording and mixing had been completed, the CD was ready to be released. The only thing it lacked was a title. Kelly wanted the title to reflect its diverse music **genres**, she told *VH1.com*:

> **"I loved the title *Pigeonhole This.* . . . It's just so funny how people try and pigeonhole you into one thing, [but] my album might as well just say, *Pigeonhole This*, 'cause you've got some rock, you've got some rock alternative type stuff, you've got a little hint of country, you've got soulful ballads and, you know, groove tracks."**

Kelly and Justin pose for a photo while promoting their 2003 film
From Justin to Kelly. **The movie was a disaster at the box office.**
"How bad is *From Justin to Kelly*?**" asked a review in** *Entertainment*
Weekly. **"Set in Miami during spring break, it's like** *Grease: The*
Next Generation **acted out by the food-court staff at SeaWorld."**

But management ruled out using *Pigeonhole This* as an album title, so Kelly suggested *Thankful*. She thought that name was a fitting way to thank the many people in her life who had helped her in her career. She even wanted to thank Simon Cowell for his harsh criticisms—because the negative comments ultimately made her work harder. The album's liner notes contain thanks to each of the *Idol* judges.

On April 15, 2003, *Thankful* was released. The song "Thankful" was a **collaboration** with the Underdogs (with Justin Timberlake) and Kenneth "Babyface" Edmonds. "You Thought Wrong" was a **duet** with former *Idol* competitor Tamyra Gray. The CD also included remixes of Kelly's debut single's two tracks, "Before Your Love," and "A Moment Like This."

Before the album came out, Kelly would admit to feeling a *little* nervous. She knew people expected a lot from her because she was the *American Idol* winner. And she also knew that the CD was coming out seven months after the first season of *Idol* had ended. Still, Kelly's girl-next-door charm remained fresh in America's minds and hearts. *Thankful* debuted at number one on the *Billboard* charts, and the record sold 297,000 copies in its first week.

Although Kelly recognized that *American Idol* boosted her first CD's sales, going forward she wanted to separate her identity from the show. She wanted more focus on Kelly Clarkson *the artist*, not Kelly Clarkson the winner of *American Idol*.

Capitalizing on *Thankful*'s immediate success, Kelly made the rounds in the spring and summer of 2003 on various television programs, including *Live with Regis & Kelly*, *The Tonight Show with Jay Leno*, and *The Late Show with David Letterman*. Around the same time she was named one of *Cosmopolitan* magazine's "Fun, Fearless Females of 2003" and one of *People* magazine's "25 Most Intriguing People."

Movie Obligation

Although Kelly had been given the opportunity to control the content and release date of her first CD, she had no control over the movie she filmed with Justin Guarini. Three weeks before its official release, in June 2003, *From Justin to Kelly* had a **premiere** screening in Kelly's hometown of Burleson, ironically, at the Cineplex where Kelly used to work. The critics panned the movie, and it was ultimately a box office failure. Kelly wasn't surprised, she told *Time*, and she explained why she did the film:

Clive Davis, the chairman and CEO of RCA Music Group, presents a plaque to Kelly that commemorates the release of her debut album in 2003. Davis, a legendary music industry executive who had discovered such stars as Whitney Houston and Alicia Keys, helped produce *Thankful*, which eventually sold more than 2.5 million copies.

"Two words: Contractually obligated! I knew when I read the script it was going to be real, real bad, but when I won, I signed that piece of paper, and I could not get out of it. Seriously, I never thought I could act, but I knew I could sing. Not to sound cocky, but I can."

Bouncing Back and Moving On

Unfazed by the negative movie reviews, Kelly concentrated even more on her music. The executives at RCA were impressed with her drive.

In July 2003 Kelly signed an agreement to appear in ads for the fashion company Candie's. Here, she unveils her first ad at a press conference in New York. "Kelly Clarkson exemplifies who the Candie's girl is, she is independent and strong minded," said company CEO Neil Cole. "She is a role model to teenage girls across America."

In a *Texas Monthly* article on Kelly, one of them described her as "a relentlessly hard worker," and added:

> **"She never once had to be told that she was going to have to keep waking up every day and proving herself. Despite all of her sudden fame, she knew what it took to break a record and establish a career: not just one television show but constant promotion and constant performing."**

One way Kelly promoted herself was by becoming a **spokesperson** for the footwear and apparel fashion company Candie's. In July she agreed to help sell the company's merchandise through a series of ads that would run that fall in fashion, entertainment, and lifestyle magazines.

That same month Kelly released her second single from *Thankful*—"Low," which she debuted in a live performance at the Nickelodeon Kids' Choice Awards. Soon after filming the video for the song, she kicked off an eight-date state fair summer tour in the Midwest.

August of 2003 would be another major milestone month for Kelly. That was when *Thankful* was certified **platinum** by the R.I.A.A. (Recording Industry Association of America, the trade group that represents the U.S. recording industry). That month she was also nominated for three MTV Video Music Awards—Best New Artist and Best Pop Video, for "Miss Independent," and the prestigious Viewer's Choice Award.

Kelly pauses for a photo at the 2003 Kids' Choice Awards show in Santa Monica, California. The year after she won the *American Idol* competition was a busy one for Kelly, and ended with her participation in another show, *World Idol*, which brought together *Idol* winners from other countries. Kelly placed second.

4

Staying Grounded

Although Kelly had found instant fame, it was important to her that she remember her roots. She made it a point to travel home to Burleson whenever she could to see friends and family. Kelly liked the fact that she could count on leaving Hollywood behind whenever she was home.

Knowing What's Important

In an interview with *Teen Tribute* Kelly explained why she continued to return home at least twice a month:

> **"It's a necessity. I have the best group of friends. We have a great support system, but they really don't care about the whole fame thing."**

That's not to say that Kelly didn't acknowledge her celebrity, nor did she forget those who inspired and helped her on her way to success. In fact, the very first thing she did with one of her paychecks was to pay back her friend Jessica. Kelly told *Teen People*:

> **"I made a joke or a bet with my—one of my girl-friends that helped me sign up for *American Idol*—that if I won *American Idol*, I'd give her a dream car. So with my check I literally went out and bought her dream car [a limited edition 1969 Corvette] and had it in a bow and showed up at her house with it."**

Kelly also took all of her hometown friends on a trip to Hawaii, bought herself a 12-acre ranch south of Fort Worth, and bought a home for her mother, Jeanne. She told the *Dallas Morning News*:

> **"I've been poor my whole life, so the fact that I'm 21 and own a house, and I got to buy my mom a house and pay her bills off—it's great that I can give back."**

Right after winning *American Idol*, Kelly indulged a bit by buying Al Pacino's massive estate in Beverly Hills, California. She then called her childhood friend Ashley Donovan to come and stay with her. Once she arrived, Ashley was quick to point out to Kelly that she was paying enough money on the house mortgage to buy a new car every month. Thanks to her hometown friend, Kelly realized that she'd made a mistake in buying the house, and she sold it. Ashley told *Texas Monthly* that success hadn't changed Kelly:

> **"[Y]ou have to understand that deep down, she still doesn't care about doing the trendy stuff, and she still says 'Cool beans,' and she still watches *Friends* like she always did."**

After Kelly sold the estate, she moved to a more modest apartment in Los Angeles, which she shares with Ashley and her brother, Jason. Kelly hired him to work as her personal assistant. That means Jason's responsible for taking Kelly to all of her appearances, handling her

Although she is an internationally known celebrity, Kelly has tried not to allow the wealth and fame that have accompanied her singing success to change the person that she is. "I'm worried that if I try to become something I'm not, then I know everything else is going to get screwed up," she told *Texas Monthly* in 2005.

managers' and agents' phone calls, accompanying her to her concerts, and taking care of her fan mail.

Back to TV

In September 2003, Kelly had a guest spot as country pop star Brenda Lee on NBC's series *American Dreams*, a television show that ran from 2002 to 2005. The drama, which was based on events of the 1960s and early 1970s, featured the popular dance show *American Bandstand*.

The following October, Kelly released *Thankful's* third single "The Trouble with Love Is." The song was featured on the soundtrack of the romantic comedy film *Love Actually*, which came out the following month. The music video *The Trouble with Love Is* debuted on Total Request Live on MTV around the same time.

Next up was a DVD entitled *Miss Independent*. It featured all of Kelly's music videos, performances of Aretha Franklin's "Respect" and

Kelly's first single from *Thankful*, "A Moment Like This," reached number one on the Billboard Hot 100 chart, and her follow-up release, "Miss Independent," was a top-10 hit. She did not fare as well with her third and fourth singles from the album, however. Neither "Low" nor "The Trouble with Love Is" made an impact on the U.S. charts.

"(You Make Me Feel Like A) Natural Woman," a **documentary** on the making of the "Low" video, live footage from the 2002 *Idol* tour, photos, and TV performance highlights. Kelly promoted "The Trouble with Love Is" and the new DVD on the *Sharon Osbourne Show* and at the American Music Awards. That Thanksgiving, Kelly once again reunited with *American Idol*, performing on the show's holiday special.

For Christmas and New Year's Day, Kelly flew to London to compete in *World Idol*, a competition involving winners of *Idol* contests from around the world. Kelly referred to the competition as the "vocal Olympics." Despite the strong competition and massive media coverage, Kelly kept a cool head and her eye on the ultimate prize—publicity. Kelly told *VH1.com*:

"It's not really about winning. It's like 'American Idol' for me, it's about showcasing myself to the world, you

know. Hopefully they'll like what I'm doing. Maybe they'll go get my CD, come to my performance. And it's all about me just having fun."

Ten other vocalists were competing for the honor of *World Idol*. Kelly placed second, behind the Norwegian *Idol* winner Kurt Nilsen.

A Grammy Nomination

Although she didn't win *World Idol*, Kelly gained another kind of recognition. Each year, the music industry (the National Academy of Recording Arts and Sciences of the United States) recognizes musicians for outstanding achievement by awarding **Grammy** Awards. In December 2003, Kelly received her first Grammy nomination, for Best Female Pop Vocal Performance in her song "Miss Independent." She told *VH1.com* her reaction when she learned about her nomination. She had been in the middle of a live radio interview, she explained:

"I just started flipping out, screaming at the top of my lungs. These people [at the radio station] were like, 'Has she never done this before? What is she doing?' But they started flipping out too. They were excited. They were the first people to hear my reaction."

The Grammy Awards ceremony is a media circus, and the red carpet is mobbed with reporters and cameramen, all snapping pictures of the stars. Who would Kelly take with her down the red carpet during the big event next year? For Kelly, the choice was simple, she told *VH1.com*:

"I'm taking my mom. I used to make her watch them [The Grammy Award programs] with me every year and she was like, 'Oh, Honey, you'll be on there one day.' And so it's cool she is going to be my date. We're getting her all dressed up and glammed up looking like a star to go down the red carpet with me."

With so many major career milestones, the year 2003 had been huge for Kelly. She had come from singing in her hometown church choir to receiving a Grammy nomination. Kelly was really achieving all that she had set out to do. And she knew bigger things lay ahead of her.

Many music critics have praised Kelly's singing ability. "Her high notes are sweet and pillowy, her growl is bone-shaking and sexy, and her midrange is amazingly confident," wrote Arion Berger in a review of *Thankful* that appeared in the influential music magazine *Rolling Stone*. "*Thankful* is testament to marketable young ladies with more talent than artistic freedom."

5

Branching Out

The year 2004 started with a bang for Kelly. Still promoting her platinum album *Thankful*, she announced that she'd be hitting the road for the "Independent" tour, a 30-city North American concert event that would run from February to April. Kelly would be sharing the stage with the second *Idol* season runner-up, Clay Aiken.

Taking Charge

At the same time Kelly kept writing new songs. Because she wanted to have more of a rock sound in her next album, she reached out to artists like guitarist Ben Moody, of the band Evanescence. Moody jumped at the chance to collaborate with Kelly. He told *VH1.com*:

> **"It's cool because [Kelly] wants to do some branching out, and I'm doing nothing but branching out. We got together and she had all these songs in mind of what she wanted to do. It's just a really, really cool process for me, because everybody is a new experience. Everybody works differently."**

Vocalist David Hodges, also formerly of Evanescence, came to help Kelly and Ben work on her songs. While working together, Kelly and David started dating, although the relationship did not last long.

Kelly's desire to move from pop to rock created some issues. RCA records chief Clive Davis and manager Simon Fuller of 19 Entertainment weren't ready to relinquish total control for the new album, which would be called *Breakaway*. Kelly told *Time*:

> **"[T]he problem was I wanted to write a lot of my own songs on *Breakaway*. Nobody else wanted me to. So there was a big ol' fight."**

Davis, a seasoned industry veteran, was skeptical about Kelly. He had seen many talented newcomers sabotage their careers by insisting on writing their own material. Sometimes it just didn't work out, and he didn't want to see that happen to Kelly. But he was willing to compromise. On her new album, Kelly would receive author or co-author credits on six of the tracks: "Because of You," "Addicted," "Breakaway," "Behind These Hazel Eyes," "Where is Your Heart," and "Hear Me."

"Breakaway"

In July, Kelly released the first single from her upcoming album. The song "Breakaway" was co-written with Avril Lavigne and producer Matthew Gerrard. Kelly considered it "autobiographical." Its lyrics tell of growing up in a small town and wanting to "take a chance, make a change," to experience more in life than was possible in a small town. "Breakaway" was featured on the soundtrack of *Princess Diaries 2: Royal Engagement*, which came out in August. The song quickly went to number one on Mainstream Top 40 radio.

The video for "Breakaway" was also released in July. Kelly had some control in the making of the video, but she once again ran into problems because her management's wishes differed from her own.

Kelly's second album, *Breakaway*, was released in November 2004. The album was an immediate hit, debuting at number three on the Billboard chart and remaining among the bestselling records all year. The album's five hit singles fueled sales. *Breakaway* eventually sold nearly 6 million copies in the United States and more than 11 million worldwide.

TV Time

In between writing, recording, and mixing, Kelly lent her voice that spring to the character of Dawn on the FOX animated series *King of the Hill*. In May she also made another trip back to *American Idol*. To help start the buzz for her upcoming record, Kelly made appearances on shows like *Live with Regis and Kelly* and *The Ellen DeGeneres Show* in the late summer and early fall. In November she reprised her role as Brenda Lee on NBC's *American Dreams*.

Kelly also performed at the *WomenRock* concert, a breast cancer fundraising event filmed in Los Angeles. The program was broadcast on the Lifetime network in October. Around that time she finally wrapped recording on *Breakaway*, and flew to Boston to sing the national anthem at the World Series.

Photographers snap shots of Kelly on the red carpet at the fifth WomenRock! Concert, an event held to raise money for breast cancer research. She sung her hit "Miss Independent" as well as a cover version of Aerosmith's "Cryin'," and joined the R&B group En Vogue in singing one of their hits.

"Since U Been Gone" marked a new direction for Kelly's music, and the critics liked where she was going. "It's a huge leap forward for the entertainer as a more confident, ever-maturing vocalist," wrote Chuck Taylor in *Billboard*. "'Gone' will elevate Clarkson to staple superstar status . . . leaving her *American Idol* victory an ever-relevant but distant memory."

"Since U Been Gone"

After Kelly decided that her next single would be "Since U Been Gone," she took the creative reins once again—against her label's wishes—to improve the song. According to *Time* magazine, Kelly hated the song's original demo, so she flew to Sweden to get the help of producers Max Martin and Lukasz Gottwald. They added more guitars and drums to the song to give it the edge that Kelly wanted. After it was released, the single became a radio smash hit. The song also helped increase anticipation for Kelly's upcoming album—and it showed her management that she was capable of creating product worth promoting.

In October, Kelly filmed the video for "Since U Been Gone," which was directed by Alex De Rakoff. In the video, she violently destroys an ex-boyfriend's apartment. Unfortunately, singing about an ex-boyfriend was timely, because her romance with David Hodges had just fizzled. Kelly posted on her Web site that their relationship had ended, but that the two would remain friends.

Kelly had not had many relationships by this point, mainly because she was so focused on her career. On her Web site, Kelly explains her requirements in a dating situation:

> **"If I date someone, I would have to date a guy who isn't intimidated by my job and how busy I am, and who isn't 'needy.' I can't handle someone who is insecure about our relationship. . . . I can't deal with someone who constantly needs reassurance."**

A Change in Management

Breakaway debuted November 30, 2004. It went to number three on the *Billboard* chart, selling 250,000 copies in its first week.

The following month, Kelly decided to part ways with Simon Fuller and 19 Entertainment. In an article with *Time*, she explained how she had been frustrated with having to fight label battles without backing or support.

> **"I'm 100% happy with my album. I just think it's funny that all these middle-age guys told me, 'You don't know how a pop song needs to sound.' I'm a 23-year-old-girl! But I was fighting those battles alone."**

Kelly signed on with a management company called The Firm. She believed the new management company would help her remap and develop her identity—and help her plot out a career that went far beyond *American Idol* fame.

"Behind These Hazel Eyes"

At the start of 2005, Kelly began to plan the Breakaway Tour, a 34-city headlining tour. At the end of March she would release a new DVD featuring new music videos and begin a North American tour, ultimately wrapping up at the end of May with a concert in British Columbia, Canada.

Kelly sports a milk mustache in this advertisement, part of the "Got Milk?" campaign. The singer admitted in a magazine interview that she was thrilled to be part of the popular, high profile campaign: "It's really cool because the people in their ads are really prominent people in what they do. I'm really happy to be a part of it."

In April, after Kelly turned 23 she decided to add more dates to the concert series. So many of her other shows had sold out that Kelly felt it was only fair to her fans that she come back around again. Her third single, "Behind These Hazel Eyes," and the accompanying video came out that April. So the tour, scheduled to run from July to September, was called the "Hazel Eyes Tour."

Toward the end of the tour, Kelly released her fourth single and video, "Because of You." The video ended up number one on MTV's TRL and VH1's New Music Radar.

Helping Out

In between tour obligations, Kelly participated in a number of benefit performances. In February 2005 she sang during the MTV Asia Aid

The year 2005 was a great year for Kelly, pictured here performing in New York's Rockefeller Plaza. She won numerous awards, including an American Music Award for Artist of the Year. She was also praised for her willingness to use her celebrity to benefit charitable causes, such as a benefit concert for the victims of Hurricane Katrina.

Benefit, held in Bangkok, Thailand. It raised money to help people affected by a devastating tsunami that had struck the region in late 2004. Between tour dates, in June, she visited the Persian Gulf as part of a four-day USO tour that performed for the troops. And in September, Kelly volunteered her voice to help raise funds for a Hurricane Katrina Benefit called "ReAct Now: Music and Relief." New Orleans had been devastated by the August 29 storm, and several other notable artists joined the lineup to help the effort.

Shortly after the "ReAct Now" show, Kelly came down with a bad case of **bronchitis**, and had to cancel five of her concert tour performances. In rescheduling them for 2006, she included a free show to make up for a sub-par performance (due to her bronchitis) for her Bay Area California fans. Kelly told *PR Newswire Association*:

> **"I love my fans and they deserve the best that I can give. I promised them I'd come back when I was healthy and I am really looking forward to making this up to them."**

A Year of Accomplishments

The awards were rolling in. That August Kelly took home two MTV Video Music Awards for "Since U Been Gone": Best Female Video and Best Pop Video. She also won Teen Choice awards for Choice Female Artist, Choice Summer Song ("Behind These Hazel Eyes"), Choice Single ("Since U Been Gone"), and Choice Album (*Breakaway*). And in November Kelly found herself the winner of two American Music Awards, for Adult Contemporary Favorite Artist and Artist of the Year.

By December of 2005, Kelly could step back and see she had accomplished a great deal since the release of *Breakaway*, just a year ago. It was the number three best-selling album of 2005, selling 4 million copies in the United States (7 million worldwide) and had been certified quadruple-platinum by the R.I.A.A. (which means it sold at least 4 million copies). Four of the album's singles—"Breakaway," "Since U Been Gone," "Behind These Hazel Eyes," and "Because of You"—had reached number one. Kelly was one of only four artists in SoundScan history to stay in the top 20 of the *Billboard* 200 for an entire year. *Breakaway* eventually sold nearly 6 million copies in the United States and more than 11 million worldwide.

WHAT GUYS SAY BEHIND YOUR BACK

Seventeen

New Year

Makeovers!

January 2006

650

Fashion Hair & Makeup Tricks!

PLUS: How To Get Your Best Body Ever!

Kelly Clarkson

"I Will Tell You Anything About Myself"

17 REAL LIFE:

SHE KILLED HER MOTHER
see page 112

EXCLUSIVE COUPONS INSIDE!

USA $2.99

Bargain Blowout
Save $$$ Shopping:

Magazine editors like to put Kelly on their covers because so many people like and admire her. Rocker Ted Leo explained her appeal in a 2006 article in *Time*: "She got where she is by having a great voice, by grinding it out and by not having an image. How can you not like that?"

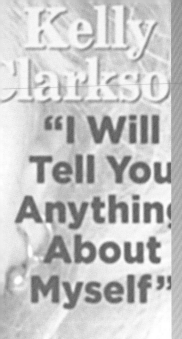

Kelly
Clarkso
"I Will
Tell You
Anything
About
Myself"

EAL LIFE:

KILLED

OTHE

page 112

6

Still Going Strong

The year 2005 had been tremendous for Kelly Clarkson. She had proven her critics wrong, wowed her record label, and won numerous awards. She had also gained more control over her career, gained confidence in her management, and finally begun to create her own identity separate from *American Idol.* She was at the top of her game.

Idol Controversy and Heartache

However, 2006 had a bumpy start. In January after a contestant on the fifth season of *American Idol* mangled a cover of Kelly's "Since U Been Gone," rumors spread that Kelly did not want to allow her songs to be used on the show.

Simon Cowell was the first to make his opinions heard on the matter. He scolded Kelly, telling *MTV News*:

> **"No matter how talented Kelly Clarkson is, she would not be in the position she's in now without winning this show. It's the public who bothered to pick up the phone to vote for her. If she refuses to give songs to be used on the show, it's like saying to every person who voted for you, 'You know what? Thank you. I'm not interested in you anymore.'"**

Kelly's management responded quickly to quell the rumors. The reps explained that Kelly was proud of her *Idol* roots and had no problem with her songs being used on the show.

February brought another major challenge, when Kelly and her rocker boyfriend Graham Colton ended their seven-month relationship. The two had been dating since July. Colton's band had been the opening act for the Hazel Eyes Tour, which meant Kelly and Graham had been able to spend a lot of time together. But later, Kelly explained to *US Weekly*, both were very busy working on other projects:

> **"[Graham] was in the studio, and we didn't even see each other. We were both like, 'This doesn't make any sense.'"**

Grammy Recognition

But Kelly had some good news in February, too. At the 2006 Grammy Awards ceremony, she won two Grammies: Best Female Pop Vocal Performance, for "Since U Been Gone," and Best Pop Vocal Album—one of the most prestigious Grammies—for *Breakaway*. Crying and shaking at the podium, Kelly gave a grateful acceptance speech, although she was later criticized for not thanking *American Idol*.

During the event Kelly also performed "Because of You," one of the first songs she'd ever written, live in front of so many of her musical idols. That opportunity made the night even more special.

Tours Abroad and at Home

Shortly after the Grammy ceremony, Kelly flew to Torino, Italy, to sing at the Olympics medal ceremony. From there she began a European leg

An excited Kelly speaks to the audience after her song "Since U Been Gone" won the Grammy Award for Best Female Pop Vocal Performance, February 2006. Kelly was a double winner that night, as *Breakaway* received a Grammy for Best Pop Vocal Album. The Grammys are the most prestigious awards in the U.S. music industry.

of her Breakaway Tour. While in the United Kingdom, Kelly installed a recording studio on her tour bus, which allowed her to start working with the band on material for her third album.

In March Kelly released her fifth and final single from *Breakaway*, the song "Walk Away." In writing the treatment for the song's music video, she had included roles for both her brother and one of her friends.

Kelly is committed to proving herself every time she performs. "I've got more than enough money," she told *Time*. "I plan on making this my life, and I want people to know I can put on a show, that I'm serious about it." Here, she sings to a crowd in Manchester, New Hampshire, during her 2006 Addicted Tour.

The following month Kelly announced plans for a third national tour. For someone who was eager to get to work on her next album, she apparently was also addicted to touring. So the perfect name for Kelly's next concert series, scheduled to hit 24 cities between June 30 and August 6, was the Addicted Tour. Kelly promised to mix her hits with brand new tracks so that fans would get a taste of what was to come on her next album.

Advertising Deals

In May, Kelly was approached by the Ford Motor Company to be a part of its "Bold Moves" campaign. The company executives wanted to create an advertising campaign that featured people who had made bold decisions in their lives, and they thought Kelly was a great example. As part of the campaign, Kelly appeared in commercials, and wrote and sang Ford's upbeat Bold Moves anthem, entitled "Go." Ford also signed on as the exclusive automotive sponsor of Kelly's upcoming Addicted Tour.

Before the Addicted Tour began, Kelly also partnered up with Glaceau Vitamin Water, in a venture to promote her favorite flavor of the beverage. She announced she would eat a more healthy diet, which meant no sodas and adhering to a strict organic diet. It was important to send her young fans the right message about eating, she told *All Headline News*:

> **"Why I love the Vitamin Water campaign is a lot of kids just down soda and it's not good. Obviously, I have a lot of young fans. I just realized that I have a platform. If you have a voice, you might as well make it a positive one."**

Not So Perfect

But Kelly would not always present a positive image. In the spring of 2006 she was wrapped up in controversy after being spotted in the audience at a concert drinking whiskey from a bottle. After being invited onstage, a visibly intoxicated Kelly danced, sung, and gestured vulgarly. A video of her "performance" was posted on numerous gossip blogs and on the video Web site YouTube.

While Kelly realizes she is often considered a role model, she wants her public to recognize that she's not perfect. Kelly told the *Seattle Times*:

> **"I used to try to be perfect and not make mistakes because I know my little nieces and girls across the world look up to me. . . . But it's not about being perfect; it's just being yourself. I'm just me. I think that's the best example I can give to them."**

Speaking Out and Helping Out

In September, Kelly took part in "Grammys on the Hill"—an event scheduled to help bring lawmakers' attention to the problem of the illegal downloading of music over the Internet. Kelly headlined the day-long event. She jammed with eight musically talented members of Congress on Capitol Hill, premiered a brand new song titled "Believe,"

Wearing the jersey of her favorite team, the Dallas Cowboys, Kelly signs autographs for fans at a November 2006 Cowboys game in Texas Stadium. Kelly remained highly visible throughout the year. In addition to her concert tours, she signed endorsement deals with Ford and Glaceau Vitamin Water to promote their products.

and was honored for her work for the Recording Academy's public education campaign.

It was not the first time Kelly has given back to others. She has served since 2004 as the Team Youth Celebrity Ambassador for the March of Dimes, which raises funds and awareness about birth defects. In the fall of 2006 she was at Hollywood's Kodak Theater for the 80th birthday party of singer Tony Bennett—a birthday celebration that also doubled as a fundraiser for an organization that provides summer camp experiences for children with serious and chronic illnesses.

In early 2007, Kelly signed a contract with the National Association for Stock Car Auto Racing to serve as a spokesperson for the 2007 season. Kelly agreed to serve as an ambassador to the sport, which means she will appear in NASCAR commercials, at charitable events, and at the end of the season awards banquet. Kelly told *MSNBC*:

Kelly meets with U.S. Senator Kay Bailey Hutchison of Texas in Washington, D.C., during the Grammys on the Hill event in September 2006. The event was sponsored by the recording industry to raise awareness about illegal downloads of digital music. During the event Kelly demonstrated the recording process for interested members of Congress.

> **"I got on board, not even for a big paycheck or anything, just to help out. Just to have fun and do some charity work with them. . . . People do stuff for money all the time. I have enough money. It's all about giving back as well."**

In April 2007, Kelly returned to her roots by appearing on *American Idol: Idol Gives Back* during a special live broadcast at the Walt Disney Concert Hall, in Los Angeles. Other stars performing at the charity

As a special ambassador for NASCAR, Kelly had the opportunity to ride around the famous track at Daytona International Speedway with stock-car champ Jimmie Johnson in February 2007. "I almost threw up!" Kelly told *People* magazine, although she quickly added, "I didn't scream or anything, so I wasn't that much of a wuss."

event included Gwen Stefani, Celine Dion, and Bono. The proceeds from *Idol Gives Back*, which amounted to more than $60 million, benefited Charity Projects Entertainment Fund, a relief organization that helps impoverished children and young people in America and Africa.

Kelly is planning to participate in Live Earth: The Concerts for a Climate in Crisis. The event is being held in order to help create awareness of environment issues around the world. It is scheduled to take place on July 7, 2007 (7/7/07), as a 24-hour multimedia simulcast concert featuring over a hundred of the world's most famous musical acts, performing on stages in seven different countries. Kelly is scheduled to perform on the U.S. stage, at Giants Stadium in New Jersey.

The Third Album

Kelly's long-awaited third album, entitled *My December*, is scheduled for release in mid-2007. Produced by David Kahne, the record features guest bassist Mike Watt on six tracks. Its first single, "Never Again," was released in late April.

Kelly has reason to be excited—for the first time in her career she has created an album in which she has written all of the songs. Kelly posted in her online journal on *KellyClarkson.com*:

> **"I can't wait for y'all to hear the album! The album is called *My December* and a few words to describe it: intimate, raw, personal, rock (although some are very sweet and soft), and I can't wait to perform every song on it! I hope y'all dig it!"**

If history is any indicator, it is likely that Kelly's incredible vocal abilities will carry her even farther than *Breakaway* did. One thing's for sure—Kelly is living proof that believing in your dreams can take you anywhere you want to go.

CHRONOLOGY

1982 Kelly Brianne Clarkson is born on April 24, in Fort Worth, Texas.

1988 Kelly's parents divorce. Kelly stays with her mother in Texas while her father moves to California.

1991 Kelly's mother, Jeanne Clarkson, marries Jimmy Taylor.

1995 Kelly's singing talent is discovered by her middle school choir teacher, who encourages the seventh grader to share her singing with others.

2000 Kelly graduates from Burleson High School.

2001 Kelly moves to Los Angeles, California, where she works with songwriter Gerry Goffin for a few months.

2002 In the spring, Kelly enters the *American Idol* competition, which she wins the following September.

Her debut single "Before Your Love/A Moment Like This" wins her a *Billboard* Award for Best Selling Single of 2002.

2003 In April Kelly's first album, *Thankful*, debuts at number one on the *Billboard* charts.

The record is certified platinum in August.

The film *From Justin to Kelly: The Rise of Two American Idols* is released in June.

That December, Kelly gets her first Grammy nomination.

2004 Kelly schedules a co-headlining tour with Clay Aiken.

She collaborates with Ben Moody and Avril Lavigne on songs for her second record.

Her singles "Breakaway" and "Since U Been Gone" become huge hits.

Thankful is certified double platinum.

Her second album, *Breakaway*, is released.

In December Kelly drops Simon Fuller and 19 Entertainment as her management and signs with The Firm.

2005 Kelly plans a major headlining tour to support *Breakaway*, which is certified quadruple platinum.

Four of the album's singles reach number one on the charts.

2006 In January Kelly is accused of not allowing *American Idol* contestants to use her songs in the competition.

She wins two Grammies: Female Vocal Performance for "Since U Been Gone" and Best Pop Vocal Album Award for *Breakaway*.

2007 The single "Never Again" is released in late April.

Kelly's third album, *My December*, is scheduled to come out in the summer.

Kelly signs on to become an ambassador for NASCAR for the 2007 season, and plans a summer tour to nearly 40 U.S. and Canadian cities.

ACCOMPLISHMENTS & AWARDS

Albums:

2003 *Thankful*

2004 *Breakaway*

2007 *My December*

Singles:

2002 "Before Your Love/A Moment Like This"

2003 "Miss Independent"
"Trouble With Love Is"
"Low"

2004 "Breakaway"

2005 "Since U Been Gone"
"Behind These Hazel Eyes"

2007 "Never Again"

Awards:

2002 American Idol Winner

Billboard Music Award for Best Selling Single:
"Before Your Love/A Moment Like This"

2005 American Music Award for Adult Contemporary
Favorite Artist

American Music Award for Artist of the Year

XM Nation Award: Pop Artist of the Year

XM Nation Award: Dashboard Anthem—Best Pop
Sing-Along, for "Since U Been Gone"

2006 Nickelodeon Kids' Choice Award for Favorite
Female Singer

MTV Asia Award for Favorite Female Artist

Teen Choice Award for Choice Music: Female Artist

American Music Award for Best Pop/Rock Female

American Music Award for Best Adult Contemporary
Artist

Grammy Award for Female Best Pop Vocal Performance,
for "Since U Been Gone"

Grammy Award for Best Pop Vocal Album, for *Breakaway*

Books

Fisher, Doris. *Kelly Clarkson*. Milwaukee: Gareth Stevens Publishing, 2007.

Tracy, Kathleen. *Kelly Clarkson*. Hockessin, Delaware: Mitchell Lane Publishers, 2007.

Magazines

Abel, Olivia et al. "Kelly Clarkson." *People*, Vol. 66, Issue 2, July 10, 2006.

Brunskill, Mary K. "Kelly Clarkson Goes Wild at Concert," *All Headline News*, August 16, 2006.

Burns, Zena. "Hot Stuff." *Teen People*, Summer Music Issue, Vol. 8, 2005.

Hollandsworth, Skip "Since She's Been Gone," *Texas Monthly*, May 2005.

"NASCAR, Kelly Clarkson Trade Fan Bases." NASCAR Wire Service, March 21, 2007.

Parsley, Aaron. "There's Something About Kelly," *Teen People*, October 28, 2005.

Tyrangiel, Josh. "Miss Independent: How Kelly Clarkson Shed her "Idol" Crown and Stole Pop Music's Throne." *Time*, February 13, 2006.

Web Sites

www.KellyClarkson.com

Kelly's official Web site contains tour dates, a personal journal, her fan club, news, video, photos and more.

www.myspace.com/KellyClarkson

Kelly's official MySpace page features song samples, photos, a blog, tour information, and video updates from Kelly herself.

http://kckellyville.com/

This Web site of Kelly's fan community is a forum where fans can meet and chat. The site also contains news, upcoming appearances, links, and photos.

www.kellyclarksonuk.com

Kelly Clarkson's official Web site for the United Kingdom features music, photos, tour dates, and appearances for Kelly in the UK.

http://www.vh1.com/artists/az/clarkson_kelly/artist.jhtml

VH1.com's Kelly Clarkson section features up-to-date news and facts about Kelly, fan forums, television appearance schedules, and more.

audition—a trial performance to test a person's abilities and skills.

bronchitis—illness that causes inflammation of air passages in the lungs that makes breathing difficult.

collaboration—working together on the same project.

debut—a first appearance or performance.

demo—short for demonstration; a recording showcasing the abilities of a musician.

documentary—a film or TV program based on facts about a historical event or person, usually supported with actual footage, photos and other authentic items.

duet—a song sung by two performers.

genre—a type, class, or category, usually referring to music.

Grammy—an annual music award given by the National Academy of Recording Arts and Sciences for outstanding achievement in the recording industry.

karaoke—a device that plays the music of songs so that the user can sing along.

pigeonhole—to assign or classify something within a limited category.

platinum—Recording Industry Association of America certification that an album has sold 1 million copies.

pop—short for popular; often referring to music with simple melodies and a danceable beat.

premiere—the first public showing of a movie.

reality TV—an unscripted television program in which people are filmed in various situations or competitions.

single—one song that is released separately from the album.

spokesperson—someone who speaks for and represents a group, brand, company, or product.

ABOUT THE AUTHOR

Michelle Lawlor is a freelance writer, graphic artist, and photographer living in central New Jersey. This is Michelle's second young adult biography. In her free time she enjoys traveling, photographing weddings and musical ensembles, and supporting the New Jersey-based band "The Frantic."

Picture Credits

page

2: RCA Records/PRNPS
6: Reuters Photo Archive
9: Splash News
11: Splash News
12: AdverMedia
15: UPI Newspictures
17: RCA Records/PRNPS
18: RCA Records/PRNPS
20: Reuters Photo Archive
22: RCA Records/PRNPS
25: Kevin Winter/KRT
27: RCA Records/NMI
28: Candie's/FPS
30: KRT/MCT

33: UPI Newspictures
34: RCA Records/PRNPS
36: Reuters Newspictures
39: RCA Records/NMI
40: KRT/MCT
41: RCA Records/PRNPS
43: Feature Photo Service
44: inkosnq-14/INFGoff
46: New Millennium Images
49: AFP
50: iPhoto
52: WireImage
53: George Bridges/MCT
54: NASCAR/FPS

Front cover: RCA Records/NMI
Back cover: Reuters Photo Archive